W9-BWT-877

DOG BREEDS

Saint Bernards

by Anne Wendorff

Consultant:
Michael Leuthner, D.V.M.
PetCare Clinic, Madison, Wisc.

BLASTOFF!
READERS
4

BELLWETHER MEDIA · MINNEAPOLIS, MN

Note to Librarians, Teachers, and Parents:

Blastoff! Readers are carefully developed by literacy experts and combine standards-based content with developmentally appropriate text.

Level 1 provides the most support through repetition of high-frequency words, light text, predictable sentence patterns, and strong visual support.

Level 2 offers early readers a bit more challenge through varied simple sentences, increased text load, and less repetition of high-frequency words.

Level 3 advances early-fluent readers toward fluency through increased text and concept load, less reliance on visuals, longer sentences, and more literary language.

Level 4 builds reading stamina by providing more text per page, increased use of punctuation, greater variation in sentence patterns, and increasingly challenging vocabulary.

Level 5 encourages children to move from "learning to read" to "reading to learn" by providing even more text, varied writing styles, and less familiar topics.

Whichever book is right for your reader, Blastoff! Readers are the perfect books to build confidence and encourage a love of reading that will last a lifetime!

This edition first published in 2010 by Bellwether Media, Inc.

No part of this publication may be reproduced in whole or in part without written permission of the publisher. For information regarding permission, write to Bellwether Media, Inc., Attention: Permissions Department, 5357 Penn Avenue South, Minneapolis, MN 55419.

Library of Congress Cataloging-in-Publication Data
Wendorff, Anne.
Saint Bernards / by Anne Wendorff.
    p. cm. – (Blastoff! Readers dog breeds)
Includes bibliographical references and index.
Summary: "Simple text and full-color photography introduce beginning readers to the characteristics of the dog breed Saint Bernards. Developed by literacy experts for students in kindergarten through third grade"–Provided by publisher.
ISBN 978-1-60014-304-5 (hardcover : alk. paper)
1. Saint Bernard dog–Juvenile literature. I. Title.
SF429.S3W46 2010
636.73–dc22
                                    2009037213

Printed in the United States of America, North Mankato, MN.
010110   1149

Contents

What Are Saint Bernards?

Saint Bernards are big **companion dogs**. They weigh between 130 and 180 pounds (59 and 82 kilograms). They are 25 to 28 inches (63 to 71 centimeters) tall. Saint Bernards have big heads and feet. Their big feet help them walk across snow. They also have big, heavy tails.

Some Saint Bernards have long hair. It can be wavy or straight. Other Saint Bernards have short hair. It is straight and thick. Saint Bernards usually have white hair. They also have **markings** on their face and body. Their markings are brown, red, or black.

fun fact

Saint Bernards drool. The amount of drool they make depends on the size of their mouth!

Saint Bernards have black faces and black ears. They often have brown eyes and wrinkles on their foreheads.

Saint Bernards have short **muzzles**, big noses, and wide nostrils. They have a strong sense of smell.

History of Saint Bernards

Saint Bernards are from the **Alps**.
The Alps are a mountain range in Europe.
The mountains are covered with snow and
are difficult to travel through.

! **fun fact**

Saint Bernards can smell
people buried under
several feet of snow.

Many people became lost in the mountains.
People trained Saint Bernards to use their
strong sense of smell to find people lost or
trapped in the snow.

Saint Bernards became famous for saving people in the Alps. Soon people in other countries wanted Saint Bernards as pets. They were brought to America to be pets in the 1800s. The **American Kennel Club (AKC)** made Saint Bernards an official **breed** in 1885.

! fun fact

The first Saint Bernards only had short hair. In the 1830s Saint Bernards were bred to grow long hair that would keep them warmer in the snow.

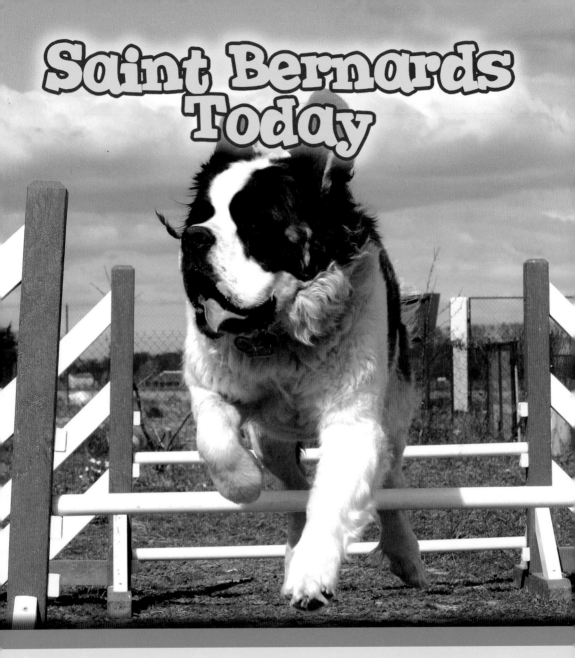

Saint Bernards Today

Saint Bernards are **working dogs**. They compete against other working dogs at dog shows. Saint Bernards are good at tracking, **agility**, and obedience events.

They are also good at search and rescue events. Saint Bernards are still used to help find people lost in the snow.

Saint Bernards also compete in cart- and sled-pulling competitions. They pull heavy carts and sleds several feet. The dog that pulls the heaviest cart or sled the fastest is the winner. Saint Bernards often win cart- and sled-pulling competitions because they are very strong.

Saint Bernards are good **guard dogs**.
They have an **instinct** to protect people.
They will bark at strangers. Their big size
may scare strangers away.

Saint Bernards are friendly, but they must be trained when they are young and small. They become too big to control and train when they get older!

Saint Bernards make good companion dogs. They can be trained to be friendly and gentle. Saint Bernards like to play with kids and adults. Would you want a Saint Bernard?

Glossary

agility—a sport where dogs run through a series of obstacles

Alps—a mountain range in Europe where Saint Bernards are from

American Kennel Club (AKC)—a group that monitors and promotes purebred dogs

breed—a type of dog

companion dogs—dogs that provide friendship to people

guard dog—a dog that barks or alerts its owner when strangers are near

instinct—a natural way to behave without being taught

markings—patterns of color in a dog's hair

muzzle—the nose, jaws, and mouth of an animal

working dog—a dog that does jobs to help people; Saint Bernards were bred to rescue people lost in the snow.

To Learn More

AT THE LIBRARY
Hall, Lynn. *Barry: The Bravest Saint Bernard*. New York, N.Y.: Random House, 2007.

Meister, Cari. *Saint Bernards*. Edina, Minn.: ABDO Publishing, 2002.

Rake, Jody. *Saint Bernards*. Mankato, Minn.: Capstone Press, 2006.

ON THE WEB
Learning more about
Saint Bernards
is as easy as 1, 2, 3.

1. Go to www.factsurfer.com.

2. Enter "Saint Bernards" into the search box.

3. Click the "Surf" button and you will see a list of related Web sites.

With factsurfer.com, finding more information is just a click away.

Index

The images in this book are reproduced through the courtesy of: Juniors Bildarchiv, front cover, pp. 4-5, 12-13, 19; Anna Yakimova, pp. 6-7; RLP Stock Photo, p. 8; Jenryk T. Kaiser, p. 9; Labat-Rouquette/Kimballstock, p. 10; Sonderegger Christof, p. 11; Bonzami Emmanuelle, p. 14; Alan and Sandy Carey, p. 15; Daneil Johnson, pp. 16-17; Gary Randall/Kimballstock, p. 18; Juan Martinez, p. 20; Darrell Lecorre, pp. 20-21.